What is MY bucket list?

This book belongs to

....

....

....

My Bucket List

100 things I want to do before I am........years old

1. _____
2. _____
3. _____
4. _____
5. _____
6. _____
7. _____
8. _____
9. _____
10. _____
11. _____
12. _____
13. _____
14. _____
15. _____
16. _____
17. _____
18. _____
19. _____
20. _____

My Bucket List

100 things I want to do before I am.......years old

21. _____
22. _____
23. _____
24. _____
25. _____
26. _____
27. _____
28. _____
29. _____
30. _____
31. _____
32. _____
33. _____
34. _____
35. _____
36. _____
37. _____
38. _____
39. _____
40. _____

My Bucket List

100 things I want to do before I am.......years old

41. _____ ☐
42. _____ ☐
43. _____ ☐
44. _____ ☐
45. _____ ☐
46. _____ ☐
47. _____ ☐
48. _____ ☐
49. _____ ☐
50. _____ ☐
51. _____ ☐
52. _____ ☐
53. _____ ☐
54. _____ ☐
55. _____ ☐
56. _____ ☐
57. _____ ☐
58. _____ ☐
59. _____ ☐
60. _____ ☐

My Bucket List

100 things I want to do before I am........years old

61. _____ ☐
62. _____ ☐
63. _____ ☐
64. _____ ☐
65. _____ ☐
66. _____ ☐
67. _____ ☐
68. _____ ☐
69. _____ ☐
70. _____ ☐
71. _____ ☐
72. _____ ☐
73. _____ ☐
74. _____ ☐
75. _____ ☐
76. _____ ☐
77. _____ ☐
78. _____ ☐
79. _____ ☐
80. _____ ☐

My Bucket List

100 things I want to do before I am.......years old

81. ☐
82. ☐
83. ☐
84. ☐
85. ☐
86. ☐
87. ☐
88. ☐
89. ☐
90. ☐
91. ☐
92. ☐
93. ☐
94. ☐
95. ☐
96. ☐
97. ☐
98. ☐
99. ☐
100. ☐

Bucket List Goal no.1

Date   /   /

Why I want this goal?

Target Date
What do I have to do to achieve this goal?

Motivate Myself

Date Achieved
What I felt when I accomplished my goal?

Bucket List Goal no.2　　　　　Date   /   /

Why I want this goal?

Target Date _____
What do I have to do to achieve this goal?

Motivate Myself

Date Achieved _____
What I felt when I accomplished my goal?

Bucket List Goal no.3   Date   /   /

Why I want this goal?

Target Date
What do I have to do to achieve this goal?

Motivate Myself

Date Achieved
What I felt when I accomplished my goal?

Bucket List Goal no.4   Date   /   /

Why I want this goal?

Target Date _____
What do I have to do to achieve this goal?

Motivate Myself

Date Achieved _____
What I felt when I accomplished my goal?

Bucket List Goal no.5   Date   /   /

Why I want this goal?

Target Date _____
What do I have to do to achieve this goal?

Motivate Myself

Date Achieved _____
What I felt when I accomplished my goal?

Bucket List Goal no.6   Date   /   /

Why I want this goal?

Target Date _____
What do I have to do to achieve this goal?

Motivate Myself

Date Achieved _____
What I felt when I accomplished my goal?

Bucket List Goal no.7   Date   /   /

Why I want this goal?

Target Date _____
What do I have to do to achieve this goal?

Motivate Myself

Date Achieved _____
What I felt when I accomplished my goal?

Bucket List Goal no.8					Date / /

Why I want this goal?

Target Date
What do I have to do to achieve this goal?

Motivate Myself

Date Achieved
What I felt when I accomplished my goal?

Bucket List Goal no.9   Date   /   /

Why I want this goal?

Target Date _____
What do I have to do to achieve this goal?

Motivate Myself

Date Achieved _____
What I felt when I accomplished my goal?

Bucket List Goal no.10   Date   /   /

Why I want this goal?

Target Date _____
What do I have to do to achieve this goal?

Motivate Myself

Date Achieved _____
What I felt when I accomplished my goal?

Bucket List Goal no.11   Date   /   /

Why I want this goal?

Target Date _____
What do I have to do to achieve this goal?

Motivate Myself

Date Achieved _____
What I felt when I accomplished my goal?

Bucket List Goal no.12   Date   /   /

Why I want this goal?

Target Date
What do I have to do to achieve this goal?

Motivate Myself

Date Achieved
What I felt when I accomplished my goal?

Bucket List Goal no.13   Date   /   /

Why I want this goal?

Target Date
What do I have to do to achieve this goal?

Motivate Myself

Date Achieved
What I felt when I accomplished my goal?

Bucket List Goal no.14   Date   /   /

Why I want this goal?

Target Date _____
What do I have to do to achieve this goal?

Motivate Myself

Date Achieved _____
What I felt when I accomplished my goal?

Bucket List Goal no.15   Date   /   /

Why I want this goal?

Target Date _____
What do I have to do to achieve this goal?

Motivate Myself

Date Achieved _____
What I felt when I accomplished my goal?

Bucket List Goal no.16   Date   /   /

Why I want this goal?

Target Date _____
What do I have to do to achieve this goal?

Motivate Myself

Date Achieved _____
What I felt when I accomplished my goal?

Bucket List Goal no.17   Date   /   /

Why I want this goal?

Target Date
What do I have to do to achieve this goal?

Motivate Myself

Date Achieved
What I felt when I accomplished my goal?

Bucket List Goal no.18   Date   /   /

Why I want this goal?

Target Date
What do I have to do to achieve this goal?

Motivate Myself

Date Achieved
What I felt when I accomplished my goal?

Bucket List Goal no.19   Date   /   /

Why I want this goal?

Target Date
What do I have to do to achieve this goal?

Motivate Myself

Date Achieved
What I felt when I accomplished my goal?

Bucket List Goal no.20   Date   /   /

Why I want this goal?

Target Date
What do I have to do to achieve this goal?

Motivate Myself

Date Achieved
What I felt when I accomplished my goal?

Bucket List Goal no.21   Date   /   /

Why I want this goal?

Target Date _____
What do I have to do to achieve this goal?

Motivate Myself

Date Achieved _____
What I felt when I accomplished my goal?

Bucket List Goal no.22   Date   /   /

Why I want this goal?

Target Date _____
What do I have to do to achieve this goal?

Motivate Myself

Date Achieved _____
What I felt when I accomplished my goal?

Bucket List Goal no.23   Date   /   /

Why I want this goal?

Target Date _____
What do I have to do to achieve this goal?

Motivate Myself

Date Achieved _____
What I felt when I accomplished my goal?

Bucket List Goal no.24   Date   /   /

Why I want this goal?

Target Date _____
What do I have to do to achieve this goal?

Motivate Myself

Date Achieved _____
What I felt when I accomplished my goal?

Bucket List Goal no.25   Date   /   /

Why I want this goal?

Target Date _____
What do I have to do to achieve this goal?

Motivate Myself

Date Achieved _____
What I felt when I accomplished my goal?

Bucket List Goal no.26   Date   /   /

Why I want this goal?

Target Date
What do I have to do to achieve this goal?

Motivate Myself

Date Achieved
What I felt when I accomplished my goal?

Bucket List Goal no.27   Date   /   /

Why I want this goal?

Target Date
What do I have to do to achieve this goal?

Motivate Myself

Date Achieved
What I felt when I accomplished my goal?

Bucket List Goal no.28   Date   /   /

Why I want this goal?

Target Date _____
What do I have to do to achieve this goal?

Motivate Myself

Date Achieved _____
What I felt when I accomplished my goal?

Bucket List Goal no.29   Date   /   /

Why I want this goal?

Target Date
What do I have to do to achieve this goal?

Motivate Myself

Date Achieved
What I felt when I accomplished my goal?

Bucket List Goal no.30   Date   /   /

Why I want this goal?

Target Date _____
What do I have to do to achieve this goal?

Motivate Myself

Date Achieved _____
What I felt when I accomplished my goal?

Bucket List Goal no.31　　　　　　Date   /   /

Why I want this goal?

Target Date _____
What do I have to do to achieve this goal?

Motivate Myself

Date Achieved _____
What I felt when I accomplished my goal?

Bucket List Goal no.32   Date   /   /

Why I want this goal?

Target Date
What do I have to do to achieve this goal?

Motivate Myself

Date Achieved
What I felt when I accomplished my goal?

Bucket List Goal no.33   Date   /   /

Why I want this goal?

Target Date _____
What do I have to do to achieve this goal?

Motivate Myself

Date Achieved _____
What I felt when I accomplished my goal?

Bucket List Goal no.34   Date   /   /

Why I want this goal?

Target Date _____
What do I have to do to achieve this goal?

Motivate Myself

Date Achieved _____
What I felt when I accomplished my goal?

Bucket List Goal no.35 　　　　　　　Date   /   /

Why I want this goal?

Target Date _____
What do I have to do to achieve this goal?

Motivate Myself

Date Achieved _____
What I felt when I accomplished my goal?

Bucket List Goal no.36   Date   /   /

Why I want this goal?

Target Date
What do I have to do to achieve this goal?

Motivate Myself

Date Achieved
What I felt when I accomplished my goal?

Bucket List Goal no.37   Date   /   /

Why I want this goal?

Target Date _____
What do I have to do to achieve this goal?

Motivate Myself

Date Achieved _____
What I felt when I accomplished my goal?

Bucket List Goal no.38   Date   /   /

Why I want this goal?

Target Date _____
What do I have to do to achieve this goal?

Motivate Myself

Date Achieved _____
What I felt when I accomplished my goal?

Bucket List Goal no.39   Date   /   /

Why I want this goal?

Target Date _____
What do I have to do to achieve this goal?

Motivate Myself

Date Achieved _____
What I felt when I accomplished my goal?

Bucket List Goal no.40   Date   /   /

Why I want this goal?

Target Date _____
What do I have to do to achieve this goal?

Motivate Myself

Date Achieved _____
What I felt when I accomplished my goal?

Bucket List Goal no.41   Date   /   /

Why I want this goal?

Target Date _____
What do I have to do to achieve this goal?

Motivate Myself

Date Achieved _____
What I felt when I accomplished my goal?

Bucket List Goal no.42   Date   /   /

Why I want this goal?

Target Date
What do I have to do to achieve this goal?

Motivate Myself

Date Achieved
What I felt when I accomplished my goal?

Bucket List Goal no.43   Date   /   /

Why I want this goal?

Target Date _____
What do I have to do to achieve this goal?

Motivate Myself

Date Achieved _____
What I felt when I accomplished my goal?

Bucket List Goal no.44   Date   /   /

Why I want this goal?

Target Date
What do I have to do to achieve this goal?

Motivate Myself

Date Achieved
What I felt when I accomplished my goal?

Bucket List Goal no.45　　　　　　Date　/　/

Why I want this goal?

Target Date _____
What do I have to do to achieve this goal?

Motivate Myself

Date Achieved _____
What I felt when I accomplished my goal?

Bucket List Goal no.46   Date   /   /

Why I want this goal?

Target Date _____
What do I have to do to achieve this goal?

Motivate Myself

Date Achieved _____
What I felt when I accomplished my goal?

Bucket List Goal no.47   Date   /   /

Why I want this goal?

Target Date
What do I have to do to achieve this goal?

Motivate Myself

Date Achieved
What I felt when I accomplished my goal?

Bucket List Goal no.48   Date   /   /

Why I want this goal?

Target Date _____
What do I have to do to achieve this goal?

Motivate Myself

Date Achieved _____
What I felt when I accomplished my goal?

Bucket List Goal no.49　　　　　　　Date   /   /

Why I want this goal?

Target Date
What do I have to do to achieve this goal?

Motivate Myself

Date Achieved
What I felt when I accomplished my goal?

Bucket List Goal no.50   Date   /   /

Why I want this goal?

Target Date
What do I have to do to achieve this goal?

Motivate Myself

Date Achieved
What I felt when I accomplished my goal?

Bucket List Goal no.51   Date   /   /

Why I want this goal?

Target Date
What do I have to do to achieve this goal?

Motivate Myself

Date Achieved
What I felt when I accomplished my goal?

Bucket List Goal no.52   Date   /   /

Why I want this goal?

Target Date _____
What do I have to do to achieve this goal?

Motivate Myself

Date Achieved _____
What I felt when I accomplished my goal?

Bucket List Goal no.53   Date   /   /

Why I want this goal?

Target Date _____
What do I have to do to achieve this goal?

Motivate Myself

Date Achieved _____
What I felt when I accomplished my goal?

Bucket List Goal no.54   Date   /   /

Why I want this goal?

Target Date _____
What do I have to do to achieve this goal?

Motivate Myself

Date Achieved _____
What I felt when I accomplished my goal?

Bucket List Goal no.55   Date   /   /

Why I want this goal?

Target Date _____
What do I have to do to achieve this goal?

Motivate Myself

Date Achieved _____
What I felt when I accomplished my goal?

Bucket List Goal no.56　　　　　Date / /

Why I want this goal?

Target Date
What do I have to do to achieve this goal?

Motivate Myself

Date Achieved
What I felt when I accomplished my goal?

Bucket List Goal no.57   Date   /   /

Why I want this goal?

Target Date _____
What do I have to do to achieve this goal?

Motivate Myself

Date Achieved _____
What I felt when I accomplished my goal?

Bucket List Goal no.58　　　　　　Date　　/　　/

Why I want this goal?

Target Date _____
What do I have to do to achieve this goal?

Motivate Myself

Date Achieved _____
What I felt when I accomplished my goal?

Bucket List Goal no.59   Date   /   /

Why I want this goal?

Target Date _____
What do I have to do to achieve this goal?

Motivate Myself

Date Achieved _____
What I felt when I accomplished my goal?

Bucket List Goal no.60   Date   /   /

Why I want this goal?

Target Date
What do I have to do to achieve this goal?

Motivate Myself

Date Achieved
What I felt when I accomplished my goal?

Bucket List Goal no.61   Date   /   /

Why I want this goal?

Target Date
What do I have to do to achieve this goal?

Motivate Myself

Date Achieved
What I felt when I accomplished my goal?

Bucket List Goal no.62　　　　　Date　/　/

Why I want this goal?

Target Date
What do I have to do to achieve this goal?

Motivate Myself

Date Achieved
What I felt when I accomplished my goal?

Bucket List Goal no.63   Date   /   /

Why I want this goal?

Target Date _____
What do I have to do to achieve this goal?

Motivate Myself

Date Achieved _____
What I felt when I accomplished my goal?

Bucket List Goal no.64   Date   /   /

Why I want this goal?

Target Date
What do I have to do to achieve this goal?

Motivate Myself

Date Achieved
What I felt when I accomplished my goal?

Bucket List Goal no.65   Date   /   /

Why I want this goal?

Target Date _____
What do I have to do to achieve this goal?

Motivate Myself

Date Achieved _____
What I felt when I accomplished my goal?

Bucket List Goal no.66   Date   /   /

Why I want this goal?

Target Date
What do I have to do to achieve this goal?

Motivate Myself

Date Achieved
What I felt when I accomplished my goal?

Bucket List Goal no.67   Date   /   /

Why I want this goal?

Target Date _____
What do I have to do to achieve this goal?

Motivate Myself

Date Achieved _____
What I felt when I accomplished my goal?

Bucket List Goal no.68   Date   /   /

Why I want this goal?

Target Date _____
What do I have to do to achieve this goal?

Motivate Myself

Date Achieved _____
What I felt when I accomplished my goal?

Bucket List Goal no.69   Date   /   /

Why I want this goal?

Target Date _____
What do I have to do to achieve this goal?

Motivate Myself

Date Achieved _____
What I felt when I accomplished my goal?

Bucket List Goal no.70   Date   /   /

Why I want this goal?

Target Date _____
What do I have to do to achieve this goal?

Motivate Myself

Date Achieved _____
What I felt when I accomplished my goal?

Bucket List Goal no.71   Date   /   /

Why I want this goal?

Target Date
What do I have to do to achieve this goal?

Motivate Myself

Date Achieved
What I felt when I accomplished my goal?

Bucket List Goal no.72   Date   /   /

Why I want this goal?

Target Date _____
What do I have to do to achieve this goal?

Motivate Myself

Date Achieved _____
What I felt when I accomplished my goal?

Bucket List Goal no.73   Date   /   /

Why I want this goal?

Target Date
What do I have to do to achieve this goal?

Motivate Myself

Date Achieved
What I felt when I accomplished my goal?

Bucket List Goal no.74　　　　　Date　/　/

Why I want this goal?

Target Date
What do I have to do to achieve this goal?

Motivate Myself

Date Achieved
What I felt when I accomplished my goal?

Bucket List Goal no.75   Date   /   /

Why I want this goal?

Target Date _____
What do I have to do to achieve this goal?

Motivate Myself

Date Achieved _____
What I felt when I accomplished my goal?

Bucket List Goal no.76   Date   /   /

Why I want this goal?

Target Date _____
What do I have to do to achieve this goal?

Motivate Myself

Date Achieved _____
What I felt when I accomplished my goal?

Bucket List Goal no.77   Date   /   /

Why I want this goal?

Target Date _____
What do I have to do to achieve this goal?

Motivate Myself

Date Achieved _____
What I felt when I accomplished my goal?

Bucket List Goal no.78　　　　　Date　/　/

Why I want this goal?

Target Date _____
What do I have to do to achieve this goal?

Motivate Myself

Date Achieved _____
What I felt when I accomplished my goal?

Bucket List Goal no.79   Date   /   /

Why I want this goal?

Target Date _____
What do I have to do to achieve this goal?

Motivate Myself

Date Achieved _____
What I felt when I accomplished my goal?

Bucket List Goal no.80   Date   /   /

Why I want this goal?

Target Date
What do I have to do to achieve this goal?

Motivate Myself

Date Achieved
What I felt when I accomplished my goal?

Bucket List Goal no.81   Date   /   /

Why I want this goal?

Target Date _____
What do I have to do to achieve this goal?

Motivate Myself

Date Achieved _____
What I felt when I accomplished my goal?

Bucket List Goal no.82   Date   /   /

Why I want this goal?

Target Date _____
What do I have to do to achieve this goal?

Motivate Myself

Date Achieved _____
What I felt when I accomplished my goal?

Bucket List Goal no.83   Date   /   /

Why I want this goal?

Target Date
What do I have to do to achieve this goal?

Motivate Myself

Date Achieved
What I felt when I accomplished my goal?

Bucket List Goal no.84　　　　　　　Date   /   /

Why I want this goal?

Target Date
What do I have to do to achieve this goal?

Motivate Myself

Date Achieved
What I felt when I accomplished my goal?

Bucket List Goal no.85   Date   /   /

Why I want this goal?

Target Date
What do I have to do to achieve this goal?

Motivate Myself

Date Achieved
What I felt when I accomplished my goal?

Bucket List Goal no.86   Date   /   /

Why I want this goal?

Target Date
What do I have to do to achieve this goal?

Motivate Myself

Date Achieved
What I felt when I accomplished my goal?

Bucket List Goal no.87   Date   /   /

Why I want this goal?

Target Date _____
What do I have to do to achieve this goal?

Motivate Myself

Date Achieved _____
What I felt when I accomplished my goal?

Bucket List Goal no.88   Date   /   /

Why I want this goal?

Target Date _____
What do I have to do to achieve this goal?

Motivate Myself

Date Achieved _____
What I felt when I accomplished my goal?

Bucket List Goal no.89   Date   /   /

Why I want this goal?

Target Date _____
What do I have to do to achieve this goal?

Motivate Myself

Date Achieved _____
What I felt when I accomplished my goal?

Bucket List Goal no.90   Date   /   /

Why I want this goal?

Target Date _____
What do I have to do to achieve this goal?

Motivate Myself

Date Achieved _____
What I felt when I accomplished my goal?

Bucket List Goal no.91   Date   /   /

Why I want this goal?

Target Date
What do I have to do to achieve this goal?

Motivate Myself

Date Achieved
What I felt when I accomplished my goal?

Bucket List Goal no.92   Date   /   /

Why I want this goal?

Target Date
What do I have to do to achieve this goal?

Motivate Myself

Date Achieved
What I felt when I accomplished my goal?

Bucket List Goal no.93   Date   /   /

Why I want this goal?

Target Date _____
What do I have to do to achieve this goal?

Motivate Myself

Date Achieved _____
What I felt when I accomplished my goal?

Bucket List Goal no.94　　　　　　Date　/　/

Why I want this goal?

Target Date _____
What do I have to do to achieve this goal?

Motivate Myself

Date Achieved _____
What I felt when I accomplished my goal?

Bucket List Goal no.95   Date   /   /

Why I want this goal?

Target Date _____
What do I have to do to achieve this goal?

Motivate Myself

Date Achieved _____
What I felt when I accomplished my goal?

Bucket List Goal no.96　　　　　　Date　/　/

Why I want this goal?

Target Date
What do I have to do to achieve this goal?

Motivate Myself

Date Achieved
What I felt when I accomplished my goal?

Bucket List Goal no.97   Date   /   /

Why I want this goal?

Target Date
What do I have to do to achieve this goal?

Motivate Myself

Date Achieved
What I felt when I accomplished my goal?

Bucket List Goal no.98					Date / /

Why I want this goal?

Target Date
What do I have to do to achieve this goal?

Motivate Myself

Date Achieved
What I felt when I accomplished my goal?

Bucket List Goal no.99   Date   /   /

Why I want this goal?

Target Date
What do I have to do to achieve this goal?

Motivate Myself

Date Achieved
What I felt when I accomplished my goal?

Bucket List Goal no.100   Date   /   /

Why I want this goal?

Target Date
What do I have to do to achieve this goal?

Motivate Myself

Date Achieved
What I felt when I accomplished my goal?

Notes

Printed in Great Britain
by Amazon